OLD GIT
WIT AND WISDOM

QUIPS AND QUOTES FOR THE YOUNG AT HEART

RICHARD BENSON

summersdale

OLD GIT WIT AND WISDOM

This revised edition copyright © Summersdale Publishers Ltd, 2017
First published in 2006
Reprinted in 2007, 2008, 2009, 2010 and 2013

Illustrations © Shutterstock

Summersdale Publishers Ltd
46 West Street
Chichester
West Sussex
PO19 1RP
UK

www.summersdale.com

Printed and bound in the Czech Republic

ISBN: 978-1-78685-059-1

Substantial discounts on bulk quantities of Summersdale
books are available to corporations, professional associations
and other organisations. For details contact general enquiries:
telephone: +44 (0) 1243 771107, fax: +44 (0) 1243 786300 or email:
enquiries@summersdale.com.

CONTENTS

EDITOR'S NOTE

Life expectancy has soared in recent years, with experts telling us that centenarians will soon be as commonplace as two-car households. Old age is here to stay – so put on your specs and pay attention!

However many golden years you've clocked up, or even if you've got it all to look forward to, there's nothing like a well-turned phrase to sum things up. In the pages that follow, well-known names from literature, screen, politics and more share their witty observations on seniority. Loveable old grumps like Winston Churchill and Bob Hope moan as only seasoned veterans of life can, while Shakespeare laments an age when one becomes 'blasted with antiquity'. But it's good to know that 'Grey Power' is hanging in there to celebrate all that makes elderliness exceptional. Philosopher Bertrand Russell ponders the advantages of white hair, while both Picasso and Brigitte Bardot talk of old age as a 'ripening'.

From advice on side-stepping the age question in the Birthdays section to priceless tips in Secrets of Longevity, this book has hilarious remarks to sweeten the pill of every aspect of old age. With contributors ranging from young'uns like Jennifer Saunders and Tom Hanks to the longest-living human being on record, Jeanne Calment (122 at the time of her death), there's something in here for you whatever your date of birth or outlook on life.

As Maurice Chevalier so aptly put it, 'old age is not so bad when you consider the alternative.'

ACCEPTING
OLD AGE

Old age is not so bad when you consider the alternative.

MAURICE CHEVALIER

What's a man's age? He must hurry more, that's all / Cram in a day what his youth took a year to hold.

ROBERT BROWNING

Old age is like a plane flying through a storm. Once you're aboard, there's nothing you can do.

GOLDA MEIR

When it comes to old age we're all in the same boat, only some of us have been aboard a little longer.

LEO PROBST

Senescence begins
And middle-age ends,
The day your descendants
Outnumber your friends.

OGDEN NASH

Eventually you will reach a point when you stop lying about your age and start bragging about it.

WILL ROGERS

GETTING OLD IS A FASCINATING THING. THE OLDER YOU GET, THE OLDER YOU WANT TO GET.

Keith Richards

At middle age the soul should be
opening up like a rose, not
closing up like a cabbage.

JOHN ANDREW HOLMES

I ALWAYS ADD A YEAR TO MYSELF,
SO I'M PREPARED FOR MY NEXT
BIRTHDAY. SO WHEN I WAS 39,
I WAS ALREADY 40.

Nicolas Cage

Don't let ageing get you down.
It's too hard to get back up.

JOHN WAGNER

I'm 59 and people call me
middle-aged. How many
118-year-old men do you know?

BARRY CRYER

Sure I'm for helping the elderly. I'm
going to be old myself some day.

LILLIAN CARTER

BENEFITS
OF OLD AGE

Old age takes away what we've
inherited and gives us what
we've earned.

GERALD BRENAN

A whole new life has opened before
you, filled with things you can think
about, study, or read about.

AGATHA CHRISTIE

'Till death do us part' doesn't sound
so horrible. It only means about 10
or 15 years and not the eternity it
used to mean.

JOY BEHAR

We don't grow older, we grow riper.

PABLO PICASSO

The age of a woman doesn't mean a thing. The best tunes are played on the oldest fiddles.

RALPH WALDO EMERSON

Old age at least gives me an excuse for not being very good at things.

THOMAS SOWELL

AUTUMN IS REALLY THE BEST OF THE SEASONS; AND I'M NOT SURE THAT OLD AGE ISN'T THE BEST PART OF LIFE.

C. S. Lewis

The more sand has escaped from the hourglass of our life, the clearer we should see through it.

NICCOLÒ MACHIAVELLI

THE GREAT THING ABOUT GETTING OLDER IS THAT YOU DON'T LOSE ALL THE OTHER AGES YOU'VE BEEN.

Madeleine L'Engle

One of the best parts of growing older? You can flirt all you like since you've become harmless.

LIZ SMITH

The great comfort of turning 49 is the realisation that you are now too old to die young.

PAUL DICKSON

You only have to survive in England and all is forgiven you.

ALAN BENNETT

One of the good things about getting older is you find you're more interesting than most of the people you meet.

LEE MARVIN

IN OLD AGE WE ARE LIKE A BATCH OF LETTERS THAT SOMEONE HAS SENT. WE ARE NO LONGER IN THE POST, WE HAVE ARRIVED.

Knut Hamsun

There's one advantage to being 102.
No peer pressure.

DENNIS WOLFBERG

At 79, if you drop something it just lies
there. At 80, people pick it up for you.

HELEN VAN SLYKE

It is sad to grow old but nice to ripen.

BRIGITTE BARDOT

The whiter my hair
becomes, the more ready
people are to believe
what I say.

Bertrand Russell

BIRTHDAYS

Age is only a number.

LEXI STARLING

BIRTHDAYS ARE GOOD FOR YOU.
STATISTICS SHOW THAT THE
PEOPLE WHO HAVE THE MOST
LIVE THE LONGEST.

Father Larry Lorenzoni

My wife hasn't had a birthday in
4 years. She was born in the year
of our Lord-only-knows.

ANONYMOUS

You're getting old when the only
thing you want for your birthday is
not to be reminded of it.

FELIX SEVERN

For all the advances in medicine,
there is still no cure for the
common birthday.

JOHN GLENN

ELDERLY
MUSINGS

Oft from shrivelled skin
comes useful counsel.

SAEMUND

ABOUT THE ONLY THING THAT COMES TO US WITHOUT EFFORT IS OLD AGE.

Gloria Pitzer

When you win, you're an old pro.
When you lose, you're an old man.

CHARLEY CONERLY

Life's tragedy is that we get old
too soon and wise too late.

BENJAMIN FRANKLIN

Nobody loves life like him
who is growing old.

SOPHOCLES

GRANDCHILDREN DON'T MAKE A MAN FEEL OLD; IT'S THE KNOWLEDGE THAT HE'S MARRIED TO A GRANDMOTHER.

G. Norman Collie

One should never make one's debut in a scandal. One should reserve that to give interest to one's old age.

OSCAR WILDE

AND IN THE END, IT'S NOT THE YEARS IN YOUR LIFE THAT COUNT. IT'S THE LIFE IN YOUR YEARS.

Anonymous

Life is a moderately good play
with a badly written third act.

TRUMAN CAPOTE

A lady of a 'certain age', which
means Certainly aged.

LORD BYRON

Anyone can get old. All you have
to do is live long enough.

GROUCHO MARX

It's true, some wines improve with age. But only if the grapes were good in the first place.

ABIGAIL VAN BUREN

Wisdom doesn't necessarily come with age. Sometimes age just shows up all by itself.

TOM WILSON

May you live all the days of your life.

JONATHAN SWIFT

By the time I have money to burn,
my fire will have burnt out.

ANONYMOUS

GROWING OLD IS LIKE BEING INCREASINGLY PENALISED FOR A CRIME YOU HAVEN'T COMMITTED.

Anthony Powell

LIFE CAN ONLY BE UNDERSTOOD BACKWARDS, BUT IT MUST BE LIVED FORWARDS.

Søren Kierkegaard

I go slower as time goes faster.

MASON COOLEY

Half our life is spent trying to find something to do with the time we have rushed through life trying to save.

WILL ROGERS

Age is something that doesn't matter, unless you are a cheese.

BILLIE BURKE

When I was young, I thought that money was the most important thing in life; now that I am old, I know it is.

OSCAR WILDE

Well enough for old folks to rise early, because they have done so many mean things all their lives they can't sleep anyhow.

MARK TWAIN

I think that what happens early on in life is that at a certain age one stands still and stagnates.

T. S. ELIOT

Old age is the verdict of life.

Amelia E. Barr

I am long on ideas, but short on
time. I expect to live to be
only about a hundred.

THOMAS EDISON

Men who are orthodox when they
are young are in danger of being
middle-aged all their lives.

WALTER LIPPMANN

Growing old is something
you do if you're lucky.

GROUCHO MARX

Old age is life's parody.

SIMONE DE BEAUVOIR

You can't turn back the clock.
But you can wind it up again.

BONNIE PRUDDEN

Life is a funny thing that happens to
you on the way to the grave.

QUENTIN CRISP

EXPERIENCE, MISTAKES AND ADVICE

If I had my life to live over again, I'd
make the same mistakes, only sooner.

TALLULAH BANKHEAD

If I had my life to live over
again, I'd be a plumber.

ALBERT EINSTEIN

The man who views the world at
50 the same as he did at 20 has
wasted 30 years of his life.

MUHAMMAD ALI

Age is a high price to
pay for maturity.

TOM STOPPARD

WE LEARN FROM EXPERIENCE
THAT MEN NEVER LEARN ANYTHING
FROM EXPERIENCE.

George Bernard Shaw

My greatest regret is not knowing at
30 what I knew about women at 60.

ARTHUR MILLER

I'll never make the mistake
of being 70 again.

CASEY STENGEL

Autumn is mellower, and
what we lose in flowers,
we more than gain in fruits.

SAMUEL BUTLER

Cherish all your happy moments: they make a fine cushion for old age.

CHRISTOPHER MORLEY

A prune is an experienced plum.

JOHN H. TRATTNER

I look carefully the second time into those things that I am most certain of the first time.

JOSH BILLINGS

I ADVISE YOU TO GO ON LIVING SOLELY TO ENRAGE THOSE WHO ARE PAYING YOUR ANNUITIES.

Voltaire

When I was young, I was told: 'You'll see when you're 50.' I'm 50 and I haven't seen a thing.

ERIK SATIE

When people tell you how young you look, they are also telling you how old you are.

CARY GRANT

Life is too short to learn German.

RICHARD PORSON

Just remember, once you're over the hill, you begin to pick up speed.

Charles M. Schulz

As I grow older, I pay less
attention to what men say.
I just watch what they do.

ANDREW CARNEGIE

Experience is a comb life gives
you after you lose your hair.

JUDITH STERN

The time to begin most
things is ten years ago.

MIGNON McLAUGHLIN

THE GOOD OLD DAYS

Most people like the old days best –
they were younger then.

ANONYMOUS

Nothing is more responsible for the
good old days than a bad memory.

FRANKLIN PIERCE ADAMS

It becomes increasingly easy, as you
get older, to drown in nostalgia.

TED KOPPEL

Sometimes when a man recalls
the good old days, he's really
thinking of his bad young days.

ANONYMOUS

THE GOOD OLD DAYS ARE NOW.

Tom Clancy

GROWING
OLD
GRACEFULLY

Let us respect grey hairs,
especially our own.

J. P. SEARS

The best mirror is an old friend.

GEORGE HERBERT

I'd like to grow very old as
slowly as possible.

IRENE MAYER SELZNICK

WHEN IT COMES TO STAYING YOUNG, A MIND-LIFT BEATS A FACE-LIFT ANY DAY.

Marty Bucella

Time may be a great healer,
but it's a lousy beautician.

ANONYMOUS

I DON'T PLAN TO GROW OLD
GRACEFULLY; I PLAN TO HAVE
FACELIFTS UNTIL MY EARS MEET.

Rita Rudner

The easiest way to diminish
the appearance of wrinkles is to
keep your glasses off when
you look in the mirror.

JOAN RIVERS

Beautiful young people are
accidents of nature, but beautiful
old people are works of art.

ELEANOR ROOSEVELT

The only real way to look younger
is not to be born so soon.

CHARLES M. SCHULZ

GRUMPINESS

There is absolutely nothing to be said in favour of growing old. There ought to be legislation against it.

PATRICK MOORE

The older a man gets, the farther he had to walk to school as a boy.

HENRY BRIGHTMAN

The older you get the stronger the wind gets – and it's always in your face.

JACK NICKLAUS

Some grow bitter with age; the more their teeth drop out, the more biting they get.

GEORGE D. PRENTICE

My Uncle Sammy was an angry man. He had printed on his tombstone: 'What are you looking at?'

MARGARET SMITH

There's a fine line between angry and grumpy. Angry isn't nice, but grumpy is funny.

RICK WAKEMAN

I refused to go on *Grumpy Old Men*. I said, 'If I go on, I will be grumpy about grumpy old men.'

STEPHEN FRY

IF OLD PEOPLE WERE TO MOBILISE EN MASSE THEY WOULD CONSTITUTE A FORMIDABLE FIGHTING FORCE.

Vera Forrester

HEALTH
AND
EXERCISE

If I'm feeling really wild I
don't floss before bedtime.

JUDITH VIORST

People who say you're just as old as
you feel are all wrong, fortunately.

RUSSELL BAKER

I am getting to an age when I can only
enjoy the last sport left. It is called
hunting for your spectacles.

EDWARD GREY

Exercise daily.
Eat wisely. Die anyway.

ANONYMOUS

TO WIN BACK MY YOUTH...
THERE IS NOTHING I WOULDN'T DO –
EXCEPT TAKE EXERCISE, GET UP
EARLY, OR BE A USEFUL MEMBER
OF THE COMMUNITY.

Oscar Wilde

Old people should not eat health foods. They need all the preservatives they can get.

ROBERT ORBEN

I've just become a pensioner so I've started saving up for my own hospital trolley.

TOM BAKER

If you rest, you rust.

HELEN HAYES

Middle age is when you
are not inclined to exercise
anything but caution.

ARTHUR MURRAY

EACH YEAR IT GROWS HARDER
TO MAKE ENDS MEET – THE ENDS
I REFER TO ARE HANDS AND FEET.

Richard Armour

I don't want a flu jab. I like getting flu. It gives me something else to complain about.

DAVID LETTERMAN

I keep fit. Every morning, I do a hundred laps of an Olympic-sized swimming pool – in a small motor launch.

PETER COOK

As for me, except for an occasional heart attack, I feel as young as I ever did.

ROBERT BENCHLEY

When you get to my age life seems little more than one long march to and from the lavatory.

John Mortimer

If I'd known I was gonna live this long,
I'd have taken better care of myself.

EUBIE BLAKE

I guess I don't so much mind being
old, as I mind being fat and old.

PETER GABRIEL

My mother is no spring chicken
although she has got as many
chemicals in her as one.

DAME EDNA EVERAGE

HOW OLD?

The older I get, the older old is.

TOM BAKER

Old age is always 15 years
older than what I am.

BERNARD BARUCH

I do wish I could tell you
my age but it's impossible.
It keeps changing all the time.

GREER GARSON

I BELIEVE IN LOYALTY; I THINK WHEN A WOMAN REACHES AN AGE SHE LIKES SHE SHOULD STICK TO IT.

Eva Gabor

Professionally, I have no age.

KATHLEEN TURNER

I'M AS OLD AS MY TONGUE AND A
LITTLE BIT OLDER THAN MY TEETH.

Kris Kringle

I was born in 1962. True. And the room next to me was 1963.

JOAN RIVERS

I am just turning 40 and taking my time about it.

HAROLD LLOYD ON TURNING 77

I refuse to admit that I am more than 52, even if that makes my children illegitimate.

NANCY ASTOR

I'm not 40 – I'm 18 with
22 years' experience.

ANONYMOUS

Whenever the talk turns to age,
I say I am 49 plus VAT.

LIONEL BLAIR

She may very well pass for 43 in the
dusk with the light behind her!

W. S. GILBERT

Age is a number –
mine is unlisted.

Anonymous

No woman should ever
be quite accurate about her age.
It looks so calculating.

OSCAR WILDE

FIRST WOMEN SUBTRACT FROM THEIR
AGE, THEN THEY DIVIDE IT, AND THEN
THEY EXTRACT ITS SQUARE ROOT.

Anonymous

IMMORTALITY

HE HAD DECIDED TO LIVE FOREVER OR DIE IN THE ATTEMPT.

Joseph Heller

The first step to eternal
life is you have to die.

CHUCK PALAHNIUK

Millions long for immortality who don't
know what to do with themselves on a
rainy Sunday afternoon.

SUSAN ERTZ

There's nothing wrong with you that
reincarnation won't cure.

JACK E. LEONARD

The only thing wrong
with immortality is that it
tends to go on forever.

HERB CAEN

If you live to be one hundred,
you've got it made. Very few
people die past that age.

GEORGE BURNS

I intend to live forever.
So far, so good.

STEPHEN WRIGHT

MEMORY
LOSS

By the time you're 80 years old you've learned everything. You only have to remember it.

GEORGE BURNS

I BELIEVE THE TRUE FUNCTION OF AGE IS MEMORY. I'M RECORDING AS FAST AS I CAN.

Rita Mae Brown

Interviewer:

CAN YOU REMEMBER ANY OF YOUR PAST LIVES?

The Dalai Lama:

AT MY AGE I HAVE A PROBLEM REMEMBERING WHAT HAPPENED YESTERDAY.

Once you've accumulated
sufficient knowledge to get by,
you're too old to remember it.

ANONYMOUS

After the age of 80, everything
reminds you of something else.

LOWELL THOMAS

As you get older three
things happen. The first is
your memory goes, and I can't
remember the other two...

NORMAN WISDOM

MIDDLE
AGE

Middle age is the awkward period when Father Time starts catching up with Mother Nature.

Harold Coffin

Middle age is when,
wherever you go on holiday,
you pack a sweater.

DENIS NORDEN

IT'S HARD TO FEEL MIDDLE-AGED,
BECAUSE HOW CAN YOU TELL HOW
LONG YOU ARE GOING TO LIVE?

Mignon McLaughlin

Middle age is when your broad
mind and narrow waist begin
to change places.

E. JOSEPH COSSMAN

Middle age is when you're old
enough to know better but still
young enough to do it.

OGDEN NASH

Middle age is when work is a lot less
fun, and fun is a lot more work.

MILTON BERLE

SETTING A GOOD EXAMPLE FOR YOUR CHILDREN TAKES ALL THE FUN OUT OF MIDDLE AGE.

William Feather

Middle age: when you begin to exchange your emotions for symptoms.

GEORGES CLEMENCEAU

MIDDLE AGE IS WHEN YOUR CLASSMATES ARE SO GREY AND WRINKLED AND BALD THEY DON'T RECOGNISE YOU.

Bennett Cerf

THE ENEMY OF SOCIETY IS MIDDLE CLASS AND THE ENEMY OF LIFE IS MIDDLE AGE.

Orson Welles

Middle age is the time in life
when, after pulling in your stomach,
you look as if you ought to
pull in your stomach.

ANONYMOUS

Middle age is when it takes
you all night to do once what once
you used to do all night.

KENNY EVERETT

Middle age is when everything new
you feel is likely to be a symptom.

LAURENCE J. PETER

The long, dull, monotonous years
of middle-aged prosperity or
middle-aged adversity are excellent
campaigning weather for the devil.

C. S. LEWIS

You know you've reached middle
age when your weightlifting consists
merely of standing up.

BOB HOPE

Mid-life crisis is that moment when
you realise your children and your
clothes are about the same age.

WILLIAM D. TAMMEUS

Spiritual sloth, or acedia, was known as The Sin of the Middle Ages. It's the sin of my middle age, too.

Mignon McLaughlin

Middle age is when you're
sitting at home on a Saturday
night and the telephone rings and
you hope it isn't for you.

OGDEN NASH

*

Middle age is when your age starts
to show around your middle.

BOB HOPE

*

Middle age – later than you think
and sooner than you expect.

EARL WILSON

If you want to recapture your youth,
just cut off his allowance.

AL BERNSTEIN

Middle age is when you choose your
cereal for the fibre, not the toy.

ANONYMOUS

Middle age is when you're faced
with two temptations and you
choose the one that will get you
home by nine o'clock.

RONALD REAGAN

THE REALLY FRIGHTENING THING ABOUT MIDDLE AGE IS THE KNOWLEDGE THAT YOU'LL GROW OUT OF IT.

Doris Day

NATURE OF OLD AGE

The first 40 years of life give us
the text: the next 30 supply
the commentary.

ARTHUR SCHOPENHAUER

As we grow older, our bodies get
shorter and our anecdotes longer.

ROBERT QUILLEN

You know you've grown up
when you become obsessed
with the thermostat.

JEFF FOXWORTHY

AS ONE GROWS OLDER, ONE BECOMES WISER AND MORE FOOLISH.

François de La Rochefoucauld

Old age means realising you will
never own all the dogs you wanted to.

JOE GORES

An old man looks permanent, as if he
had been born an old man.

H. E. BATES

Old age is when you
resent the swimsuit issue of Sports
Illustrated because there are
fewer articles to read.

GEORGE BURNS

Forty is the old age of youth, fifty is the youth of old age.

French Proverb

Time and trouble will tame
an advanced young woman,
but an advanced old woman is
uncontrollable by any earthly force.

DOROTHY L. SAYERS

Growing old is no more than
a bad habit, which a busy person
has no time to form.

ANDRÉ MAUROIS

Age seldom arrives smoothly or
quickly. It's more often a
succession of jerks.

JEAN RHYS

THE ESSENCE OF AGE IS INTELLECT. WHEREVER THAT APPEARS, WE CALL IT OLD.

Ralph Waldo Emerson

NOT GROWING UP

It takes a long time to
grow young.

PABLO PICASSO

LIFE WOULD BE INFINITELY HAPPIER
IF WE COULD ONLY BE BORN AT
THE AGE OF 80 AND GRADUALLY
APPROACH 18.

Mark Twain

YOU'RE ONLY YOUNG ONCE, BUT YOU CAN BE IMMATURE FOREVER.

Germaine Greer

Age does not diminish the extreme disappointment of having a scoop of ice cream fall from the cone.

JIM FIEBIG

The surprising thing about young fools is how many survive to become old fools.

DOUG LARSON

Growing old is compulsory.
Growing up is optional.

BOB MONKHOUSE

The secret of genius is to carry the spirit of the child into old age, which means never losing your enthusiasm.

ALDOUS HUXLEY

THE TRAGEDY OF OLD AGE IS NOT THAT ONE IS OLD, BUT THAT ONE IS YOUNG.

Oscar Wilde

I've got to go and see the old folk.

The Queen Mother at age 97, spotting a group of pensioners at Cheltenham Racecourse

Inside every older person is
a younger person wondering
what the hell happened.

CORA HARVEY ARMSTRONG

I PLAN ON GROWING OLD
MUCH LATER IN LIFE, OR
MAYBE NOT AT ALL.

Patty Carey

FIFTY IS THE NEW 34.

Tom Hanks

Few people know how to be old.

MAGGIE KUHN

WHEN THEY TELL ME I'M
TOO OLD TO DO SOMETHING,
I ATTEMPT IT IMMEDIATELY.

Pablo Picasso

PLEASURES OF OLD AGE

W. C. Fields has a profound respect for old age. Especially when it's bottled.

GENE FOWLER

MY GRANDMOTHER IS OVER 80 AND STILL DOESN'T NEED GLASSES. DRINKS RIGHT OUT OF THE BOTTLE.

Henny Youngman

When you get to 52 food becomes
more important than sex.

PRUE LEITH

One of the many pleasures of
old age is giving things up.

MALCOLM MUGGERIDGE

I smoke 10 to 15 cigars a day; at my
age I have to hold on to something.

GEORGE BURNS

Jameson's Irish Whiskey really does improve with age: the older I get the more I like it.

BOB MONKHOUSE

I'M AT THE AGE WHERE FOOD HAS TAKEN THE PLACE OF SEX IN MY LIFE.

Rodney Dangerfield

PHYSICAL
EFFECTS

You know you're getting old
when everything hurts. And what
doesn't hurt doesn't work.

HY GARDNER

YOU DON'T KNOW REAL
EMBARRASSMENT UNTIL YOUR HIP
SETS OFF A METAL DETECTOR.

Ross McGuinness

Is not your voice broken, your wind short, your chin double, your wit single, and every part about you blasted with antiquity?

William Shakespeare

I don't want to end up in an old folks' home wearing incompetence pads. I'm still compost mentis.

HARRIET WYNN

Many of us are at the 'metallic' age – gold in our teeth, silver in our hair, and lead in our pants.

ANONYMOUS

Advanced old age is when you sit in a rocking chair and can't get it going.

ELIAKIM KATZ

They say that age is all in your
mind. The trick is keeping it from
creeping down into your body.

ANONYMOUS

I knew I was going bald when
it was taking longer and longer
to wash my face.

HARRY HILL

Life begins at 40 – but so
do fallen arches, rheumatism
and faulty eyesight.

HELEN ROWLAND

I DON'T NEED YOU TO REMIND ME OF MY AGE, I HAVE A BLADDER TO DO THAT FOR ME.

Stephen Fry

My friend George has false
teeth – with braces on them.

STEVEN WRIGHT

I DON'T FEEL 80. IN FACT I DON'T
FEEL ANYTHING UNTIL NOON, THEN
IT'S TIME FOR MY NAP.

Bob Hope

EVERYTHING SLOWS DOWN WITH AGE, EXCEPT THE TIME IT TAKES CAKE AND ICE CREAM TO REACH YOUR HIPS.

John Wagner

Wrinkles should merely indicate where smiles have been.

Mark Twain

Thirty-five is when you finally get your head together and your body starts falling apart.

CARYN LESCHEN

After a certain number of years our faces become our biographies.

CYNTHIA OZICK

Thoughtfulness begets wrinkles.

CHARLES DICKENS

LIKE A LOT OF FELLOWS AROUND HERE, I HAVE A FURNITURE PROBLEM. MY CHEST HAS FALLEN INTO MY DRAWERS.

Billy Casper

I had a job selling hearing aids
from door to door. It wasn't easy,
because your best prospects
never answered.

BOB MONKHOUSE

BEAUTY AND UGLINESS DISAPPEAR
EQUALLY UNDER THE WRINKLES OF
AGE; ONE IS LOST IN THEM, THE
OTHER HIDDEN.

Jonathan Petit Senn

Alas, after a certain age every
man is responsible for his face.

ALBERT CAMUS

I'm at an age where my back
goes out more than I do.

PHYLLIS DILLER

I used to think I'd like less
grey hair. Now I'd like more of it.

RICHIE BENAUD

RETIREMENT

People ought to retire at 40 when they feel over-used and go back to work at 65 when they feel useless.

Sister Carol Anne O'Marie

Retired is being tired twice… first tired of working, then tired of not.

RICHARD ARMOUR

It's very hard to make a home for a man if he's always in it.

WINIFRED KIRKLAND

I don't want to retire. I'm not that good at crossword puzzles.

NORMAN MAILER

When men reach their sixties and retire, they go to pieces. Women go right on cooking.

GAIL SHEEHY

MY PARENTS LIVE IN A RETIREMENT COMMUNITY, WHICH IS BASICALLY A MINIMUM-SECURITY PRISON WITH A GOLF COURSE.

Joel Warshaw

WHEN A MAN RETIRES HIS WIFE GETS TWICE THE HUSBAND BUT ONLY HALF THE INCOME.

Chi Chi Rodriguez

When a man falls into his anecdotage, it is a sign for him to retire from the world.

BENJAMIN DISRAELI

The best time to start thinking about your retirement is before the boss does.

ANONYMOUS

Don't retire, retread!

ROBERT K. OTTERBOURG

The trouble with retirement is that
you never get a day off.

ABE LEMONS

I'm 42 around the chest, 52 around
the waist, 92 around the golf course
and a nuisance around the house.

GROUCHO MARX

Once it was impossible to
find any Bond villains older
than myself, I retired.

ROGER MOORE

SECRETS OF LONGEVITY

The secret of staying young is to
live honestly, eat slowly and
lie about your age.

LUCILLE BALL

Interviewer: 'You've reached
the ripe old age of 121. What do
you expect the future will be like?'
'Very short.'

JEANNE CALMENT

My first advice on how not to
grow old would be to choose
your ancestors carefully.

BERTRAND RUSSELL

EVERY ONE DESIRES TO LIVE LONG, BUT NO ONE WOULD BE OLD.

Jonathan Swift

The fountain of youth is a mixture
of gin and vermouth.

COLE PORTER

Old age is like everything else.
To make a success of it, you've
got to start young.

THEODORE ROOSEVELT

The trick is growing up
without growing old.

CASEY STENGEL

Ageing seems to be the only available way to live a long life.

DANIEL FRANCOIS ESPRIT AUBER

THE IDEA IS TO DIE YOUNG AS LATE AS POSSIBLE.

Ashley Montagu

A man's only as old as the
woman he feels.

GROUCHO MARX

I'll tell ya how to stay young: hang
around with older people.

BOB HOPE

Age is a question of mind over matter.
If you don't mind, it doesn't matter!

MARK TWAIN

**Since people
are going to be living
longer and getting older,
they'll just have to learn
how to be babies longer.**

Andy Warhol

To stop ageing – keep on raging.
MICHAEL FORBES

More people would live to a ripe
old age if they weren't too
busy providing for it.
ANONYMOUS

Old age is no place for sissies.
BETTE DAVIS

SENILITY

I AM IN THE PRIME
OF SENILITY.

Benjamin Franklin

How the hell should I know? Most of the people my age are dead. You could look it up.

They say that after the age of 20 you lose 50,000 brain cells a day. I think it's much more.

NED SHERRIN

My experience is that as soon as people are old enough to know better, they don't know anything at all.

OSCAR WILDE

SEX AND INDECENCY

OLD AGE IS AN EXCELLENT TIME FOR OUTRAGE. MY GOAL IS TO SAY OR DO AT LEAST ONE OUTRAGEOUS THING EVERY WEEK.

Maggie Kuhn

Don't worry about avoiding
temptation – as you grow older,
it starts avoiding you.

WINSTON CHURCHILL

SEX MANUAL FOR THE MORE
MATURE: 'HOW TO TELL AN ORGASM
FROM A HEART ATTACK!'

Anonymous

I can still enjoy sex at 75.
I live at 76, so it's no distance.

BOB MONKHOUSE

The older one grows, the
more one likes indecency.

VIRGINIA WOOLF

I'm 78 but I still use a condom when I
have sex. I can't take the damp.

ALAN GREGORY

No matter. The dead bird does not fall out of the nest.

Winston Churchill after being told his flies were undone

Middle age is when
a guy keeps turning off the
lights for economical rather
than romantic reasons.

LILLIAN CARTER

WHAT MOST PERSONS CONSIDER AS
VIRTUE, AFTER THE AGE OF 40 IS
SIMPLY A LOSS OF ENERGY.

Voltaire

After a man passes 60, his
mischief is mainly in his head.

EDGAR WATSON HOWE

Old age likes indecency.
It's a sign of life.

MASON COOLEY

Now that I'm 78, I do Tantric
sex because it's very slow.

JOHN MORTIMER

Talk about getting old. I was getting dressed and a peeping tom looked in the window, took a look and pulled down the shade.

JOAN RIVERS

THERE IS NO PLEASURE WORTH FORGOING JUST FOR AN EXTRA THREE YEARS IN THE GERIATRIC WARD.

John Mortimer

SIGNS OF
OLD AGE

The ageing process has you
firmly in its grasp if you never get
the urge to throw a snowball.

DOUG LARSON

It's a sign of age if you feel like the
morning after the night before and
you haven't been anywhere.

ANONYMOUS

Grandmother, as she gets older,
is not fading, but becoming
more concentrated.

PAULETTE ALDEN

YOU KNOW YOU'RE OLD IF THEY HAVE DISCONTINUED YOUR BLOOD TYPE.

Phyllis Diller

You're an old-timer if you can remember when setting the world on fire was a figure of speech.

FRANKLIN P. JONES

YOU KNOW YOU ARE GETTING OLD WHEN THE CANDLES COST MORE THAN THE CAKE.

Bob Hope

One day you look in the mirror
and realise the face you are
shaving is your father's.

ROBERT HARRIS

Old age is when the liver spots
show through your gloves.

PHYLLIS DILLER

A man loses his illusions first, his
teeth second, and his follies last.

HELEN ROWLAND

THERE IS ONLY ONE CURE FOR GREY. IT WAS INVENTED BY A FRENCHMAN. IT IS CALLED THE GUILLOTINE.

P. G. Wodehouse

Old age comes on suddenly, and not gradually as is first thought.

EMILY DICKINSON

I'M GETTING ON. I'M NOW EQUIPPED WITH A SNOOZE BUTTON.

Denis Norden

You know you're getting old
when your idea of a hot, flaming
desire is a barbecued steak.

VICTORIA FABIANO

The first sign of maturity
is the discovery that the volume
knob also turns to the left.

JERRY M. WRIGHT

You know you're getting old
when all the names in your black
book have M.D. after them.

ARNOLD PALMER

You're not old until it takes you longer to rest up than it does to get tired.

PHOG ALLEN

YOU KNOW YOU'RE GETTING OLDER IF YOU HAVE MORE FINGERS THAN REAL TEETH.

Rodney Dangerfield

STYLE

If you really want to annoy your glamorous, well-preserved 42-year-old auntie, say, 'I bet you were really pretty when you were young.'

LILY SAVAGE

My dad's pants kept creeping up on him. By 65 he was just a pair of pants and a head.

JEFF ALTMAN

You know you're getting old when you're dashing through Marks and Spencer's, spot a pair of Dr Scholl's sandals, stop, and think, hmm, they look comfy.

VICTORIA WOOD

TALKING 'BOUT THE GENERATIONS

There are three stages in an actor's career: Who is John Amos? Get me John Amos. Get me a young John Amos.

John Amos

Parents often talk about the younger generation as if they didn't have anything to do with it.

HAIM GINOTT

Wrinkles are hereditary. Parents get them from their children.

DORIS DAY

Young people tell what they are doing, old people what they have done and fools what they wish to do.

FRENCH PROVERB

Why do grandparents and grandchildren get along so well? They have the same enemy – the mother.

CLAUDETTE COLBERT

WHEN YOU ARE ABOUT 35 YEARS OLD, SOMETHING TERRIBLE ALWAYS HAPPENS TO MUSIC.

Steve Race

It's hard for me to get used to these changing times. I can remember when the air was clean and sex was dirty.

GEORGE BURNS

There are three periods in life: youth, middle age and 'how well you look'.

NELSON ROCKEFELLER

Youth is the time of getting, middle age of improving, and old age of spending.

ANNE BRADSTREET

THE FIRST HALF OF OUR LIFE IS RUINED BY OUR PARENTS — AND THE SECOND HALF BY OUR CHILDREN.

Clarence Darrow

No matter how old a mother is she watches her middle-aged children for signs of improvement.

FLORIDA SCOTT-MAXWELL

The children despise their parents until the age of 40, when they suddenly become just like them – thus preserving the system.

QUENTIN CREWE ON THE BRITISH UPPER CLASSES

Be kind to your kids, they'll be choosing your nursing home.

ANONYMOUS

There are only three ages for women
in Hollywood – Babe, District
Attorney, and Driving Miss Daisy.

GOLDIE HAWN

My nan said, 'What do you
mean when you say the computer
went down on you?'

JOSEPH LONGTHORNE

At 20 years of age the will reigns;
at 30 the wit; at 40 the judgement.

BENJAMIN FRANKLIN

THOUGHTS ON DEATH AND AFTERLIFE

Since I got to 80, I've started reading
the Bible a lot more. It's kind of like
cramming for my finals.

VINCENT WATSON

He's so old that when he
orders a three-minute egg, they
ask for the money up front.

MILTON BERLE

I want to die young at
an advanced age.

MAX LERNER

WHEN I GET IN A TAXI, THE FIRST THING THEY SAY IS, 'HELLO ERIC, I THOUGHT YOU WERE DEAD.'

Eric Sykes

In Liverpool, the difference
between a funeral and a wedding
is one less drunk.

PAUL O'GRADY

If you die in an elevator, be
sure to push the Up button.

SAM LEVENSON

If you die in an elevator, be

Memorial services are the cocktail
parties of the geriatric set.

HAROLD MACMILLAN

My grandmother was a very tough woman. She buried three husbands and two of them were just napping.

RITA RUDNER

I DON'T MIND DYING. TROUBLE IS, YOU FEEL SO BLOODY STIFF THE NEXT DAY.

George Axelrod

I know I can't cheat death,
butI can cheat old age.

DARWIN DEASON

My old mam reads the obituary
page everyday but she could never
understand how people always
die in alphabetical order.

FRANK CARSON

Death is life's way of
telling you you're fired.

ANONYMOUS

No one is so old as to think he cannot live one more year.

CICERO

I am ready to meet my Maker. Whether my Maker is ready for the ordeal of meeting me is another matter.

WINSTON CHURCHILL

We think he's dead, but we're afraid to ask.

ANONYMOUS COMMITTEE MEMBER REFERRING TO THE 79-YEAR-OLD CHAIRMAN OF HOUSE COMMITTEE, WASHINGTON, 1984

If you think nobody cares whether you are alive or dead, try missing a couple of car payments.

Ann Landers

WOMEN AND MEN

Trouble is, by the time you
can read a girl like a book, your
library card has expired.

MILTON BERLE

Few women admit their age.
Few men act theirs.

ANONYMOUS

An archaeologist is the best husband
a woman can have. The older she gets
the more interested he is in her.

AGATHA CHRISTIE

WOMEN ARE NOT FORGIVEN FOR AGEING. ROBERT REDFORD'S LINES OF DISTINCTION ARE MY OLD-AGE WRINKLES.

Jane Fonda

My husband's idea of a good
night out is a good night in.

MAUREEN LIPMAN

THE BEST YEARS OF A
WOMAN'S LIFE – THE TEN YEARS
BETWEEN 39 AND 40.

Anonymous

The lovely thing about being
40 is that you can appreciate
25-year-old men.

COLLEEN McCULLOUGH

When women enter middle age,
it gives men a pause.

ANONYMOUS

A woman's always younger
than a man of equal years.

ELIZABETH BARRETT BROWNING

A woman is as old as she
looks before breakfast.

EDGAR WATSON HOWE

WHEN I PASSED 40 I DROPPED
PRETENCE, 'CAUSE MEN LIKE WOMEN
WHO GOT SOME SENSE.

Maya Angelou

Whatever you may look like, marry a
man your own age – as your beauty
fades, so will his eyesight.

PHYLLIS DILLER

The best way to get a husband
to do anything is to suggest
that he is too old to do it.

FELICITY PARKER

Age to women is like
Kryptonite to Superman.

KATHY LETTE

YOUTH V OLD AGE

THE OLD BEGIN TO COMPLAIN OF THE CONDUCT OF THE YOUNG WHEN THEY THEMSELVES ARE NO LONGER ABLE TO SET A BAD EXAMPLE.

François de La Rochefoucauld

An old timer is one who remembers
when we counted our blessings
instead of our calories.

ANONYMOUS

I am not young enough to
know everything.

OSCAR WILDE

Youth is a wonderful thing. What a
crime to waste it on children.

GEORGE BERNARD SHAW

A man has reached middle age when he is warned to slow down by his doctor instead of the police.

ANONYMOUS

I have now gotten to the age when I must prove that I'm just as good as I never was.

REX HARRISON

Young men want to be faithful, and are not; old men want to be faithless, and cannot.

OSCAR WILDE

I never dared
to be radical when
young for fear it would
make me conservative
when old.

Robert Frost

The elderly don't drive that badly;
they're just the only ones with
time to do the speed limit.

JASON LOVE

IN YOUTH WE TEND TO LOOK
FORWARD; IN OLD AGE WE TEND
TO LOOK BACK; IN MIDDLE AGE
WE TEND TO LOOK WORRIED.

Anonymous

Young people don't know
what age is, and old people
forget what youth was.

IRISH PROVERB

The young man knows the rules but
the old man knows the exceptions.

OLIVER WENDELL HOLMES

In youth, we ran into difficulties, in
old age difficulties run into us.

JOSH BILLINGS

I HAVE EVERYTHING I HAD 20 YEARS AGO, ONLY IT'S ALL A LITTLE BIT LOWER.

Gypsy Rose Lee

In youth the days are short and the years are long; in old age the years are short and the days are long.

NIKITA IVANOVICH PANIN

The old age of an eagle is better than the youth of a sparrow.

PROVERB

One of the many things nobody ever tells you about middle age is that it's a nice change from being young.

WILLIAM FEATHER

The old believe everything;
the middle-aged suspect everything;
the young know everything.

OSCAR WILDE

Youth would be an ideal state
if it came a little later in life.

H. H. ASQUITH

Age is not different from earlier life
as long as you're sitting down.

MALCOLM COWLEY

PEOPLE WANT YOU TO BE LIKE YOU WERE IN 1969. THEY WANT YOU TO, BECAUSE OTHERWISE THEIR YOUTH GOES WITH YOU.

Mick Jagger

Boys will be boys and so will a
lot of middle-aged men.

KIN HUBBARD

Youth is when you're allowed to stay
up late on New Year's Eve. Middle age
is when you're forced to.

BILL VAUGHN

One day a bachelor, the next a grampa.
What is the secret of the trick?
How did I get so old so quick?

OGDEN NASH

When you
are dissatisfied and
would like to go back
to your youth...
think of algebra.

Will Rogers

If you're interested in finding out more
about our books, find us on Facebook
at Summersdale Publishers and follow
us on Twitter at @Summersdale.

www.summersdale.com